WHERE DID YOU LEAVE JESUS?

WHERE DID YOU LEAVE JESUS?

In Your Life As A Christian

MARY ANN SULLIVAN

Purelilly Press

First Printing, 2024

ISBN: 979-8-9879012-8-1

Published by Purelilly Press Publishing
Huntsville, Texas

A Special Dedication

To a very special man of God

Dr. J.E. Murdock
President and founder of
Highway and Hedges Ministries
An organization devoted to building churches.

Dr. Murdock is the father of Mike Murdock, the great wisdom teacher and songwriter. While visiting with Dr. J.E. following one of Mike's classes, he revealed this revelation the Lord had given him.

"IT COULD HAPPEN TO ANYONE"
Anyone can lose Jesus.
His own mother did!

I asked him if I could use it in a book. He said, "You certainly may."

Also

Dedicated to everyone who ever searched for Jesus,
maybe not knowing exactly how or where to look,
finding out he is always right where you left him.

His word says, "I will never leave you nor forsake you."
So, he didn't leave...we did! Thus, the question...

"WHERE DID YOU LEAVE JESUS?"

First of all, let me thank Mike Murdock. In his wonderful books on WISDOM, Mike always lets the reader know why he wrote the book. I would like to do the same.

I wrote this book for everyone who has come to know Jesus and, for some reason, "left" him along the way. You can be sure he is right where you left him.

Also, I hope anyone who has never known Jesus will want to know him after reading this book. The Bible promises, "Seek, and you shall find."

So, whether you knew him and left him, or you have not met him yet, seek him with all your heart.

The rewards are immense!

CONTENTS

MANGER

Where did you leave Jesus?

Did you leave him in the MANGER?

I don't know about you, but when the Holy Spirit begins to speak to me, I can't help but listen. Early one morning, I heard him ask me, "Where did you leave, Jesus?"

I replied, "What, Lord?"

Again, I heard him ask, "WHERE DID YOU LEAVE JESUS? W.D.Y.L.J."

Answering puzzled, I said, "I don't know."

I pondered and asked myself, and now I ask you, "Well, did you leave him in the manger, just another baby?" You might think, "He's real cute and sweet, but babies can't do much. I'll spend time with him when he gets older."

And she brought forth her firstborn son, and wrapped him in swaddling clothes, and laid him in a manger...

Luke 2:7

For unto you is born this day in the city of David a Saviour, which is Christ the Lord.

Luke 2:11

TEMPLE

Where did you leave Jesus?

Did you leave him at the TEMPLE?

"IT COULD HAPPEN TO ANYONE."

EVEN HIS MOTHER LEFT HIM!

Oh yes! Mary and Joseph traveled to Jerusalem every year for the Feast of the Passover. As they traveled home from Jerusalem, unbeknownst to them, Jesus stayed behind in the temple. At the time, he was twelve, and she thought he was with relatives and friends in the caravan. When they began looking for Jesus, he was nowhere to be found. Returning to Jerusalem, she and Joseph found him there in the temple.

Do you worship Jesus in "God's house" and then leave him there when you go home?

And when they had fulfilled the days, as they returned, the child Jesus tarried behind in Jerusalem; and Joseph and his mother knew not of it.

Luke 2:43

And when they found him not, they turned back again to Jerusalem seeking him. And it came to pass, that after three days they found him in the temple, sitting in the midst of the doctors, both hearing them, and asking them questions.

Luke 2:45-46

How about you? Have you traveled on, leaving Jesus to be about the Father's business?

And all that heard him were astonished at his understanding and answers. And when they saw him, they were amazed: and his mother said unto him, Son, why hast thou thus dealt with us? Behold, thy father and I have sought thee sorrowing.

And he said unto them, How is it that you sought me? Wist ye not that I must be about my Father's business?

Luke 2:47-49

I believe Jesus, as our example, is telling us that we are never too young to be about God's business. It is the most important thing we will do while here on this earth. Jesus's parents lost him for three days while he was at the temple.

How often do you lose him?

Take him everywhere you go. He was about his Father's business. If you are about his Father's business, he WILL be there. He promised, "I will never leave you nor forsake you."

NAZARETH

Where did you leave Jesus?

Did you leave him in NAZARETH?

Maybe you left him in Nazareth, the place where Jesus grew up, possibly thinking of him as just a carpenter's son.

> *And he came to Nazareth, where he had been brought up: and as his custom was, he went into the synagogue on the Sabbath day, stood up for to read.*
>
> *And all bare witness, and wondered at the gracious words which proceeded out of his mouth. And they said, Is not this Joseph's son?*
>
> *And he said, Verily I say unto you, No prophet is accepted in his own country.*
>
> Luke 4:16, 22, 24

Jesus was not only the son of a carpenter. Jesus, as the Incarnate son of God, was, and is, the "exact" representation of God's "nature and character." That is exactly what he wants you to be.

THE WELL

Where did you leave Jesus?

Could it be you left him at THE WELL?

L ike the Samaritan woman, you feel unworthy for Jesus to speak to you. You've made so many mistakes that you feel like Jesus can't or won't help you. *Maybe he has something for everyone else, but surely not for me. And besides, no one has ever just given me anything.*

Jacob's well was there, and Jesus, tired as he was from the journey, sat down by the well. It was about the sixth hour. When a Samaritan woman came to draw water, Jesus said to her "Will you give me a drink" (his disciples had gone to buy food).

The Samaritan woman said to him, You are a Jew and I am a Samaritan woman. How can you ask me for a drink? (for Jews do not associate with Samaritans.)

John 4:6-9

In the book of John, Jesus cautions all to partake of him. For only he can satisfy.

Jesus answered, Everyone who drinks this water will be thirsty again, But whoever drinks the water I give him will never thirst. Indeed, the water I give him will become in him a spring of water welling up to eternal life.

The woman said to him, Sir, give me this water so that I won't get thirsty and have to keep coming here to draw water.

John 4:13-15

Do not let the shame of past mistakes cause you to leave Jesus. Remember, Jesus said, "everyone," and that includes you. He is the one TRUE answer to everything we long for. Develop a thirst for Jesus, not the water of this world.

VALLEY OF INDECISION

Where did you leave Jesus?

Perhaps you left him in the
VALLEY of INDECISION.

Ask yourself, "Can I really do this? Can I turn my back on the world and follow Jesus full steam, with all my heart, not looking back?"

And there went great multitudes with him: and he turned, and said unto them, If any man come to me, and hate not his father, and mother, and wife, and children, and brethren, and sisters, yea, and his own life also, he cannot be my disciple. And whosoever doth not bear his cross, and come after me cannot be my disciple. For which of you, intending to build a tower, sitteth not down first, and counteth the cost, whether he have sufficient to finish it?

Luke 14:25-28

Jesus cannot use you in a "double-minded" nature. You cannot live one day in the world, and the next day, live for Jesus. You must make up your mind about who and what you will serve. It will be one or the other, Jesus or the world.

So likewise, whosoever he be of you that forsaketh not all that he hath, he cannot be my disciple. Salt is good: but if the salt have lost his savor, wherewith shall it be seasoned?

Luke 14:33-34"

Why not strive to get out of the valley of indecision and onto the mountaintop of victory in the Lord Jesus? When you count the cost and give your all for Jesus, he will not leave you nor forsake you.

There is complete victory in Jesus. He has already defeated the world. It was done at Calvary, and in him, you also are the victor. Why would anyone trade victory for defeat?

GATE CALLED STRAIT

Where did you leave Jesus?

Maybe you left him at the
GATE CALLED STRAIT.

D id you not know he is calling you to enter in before it is
too late?

*And he went through the cities and villages, teaching and
journeying toward Jerusalem. Then said one unto him,
Lord, are there few that be saved?*

*And he said unto them, Strive to enter in at the straight gate:
for many, I say unto you will seek to enter in, and shall not
be able. When once the master of the house is risen up, and
hath shut the door, and ye begin to stand without, and to
knock at the door, saying, Lord, open up to us; and he shall
answer and say unto you, I know you not whence ye are:...*

Luke 13:22-25

Think about it very seriously, for there will come a time
when it will be too late. Jesus pleads to each of us to accept his
sacrifice and his invitation to come in.

When the door is closed, it will be closed permanently.
There will be no way to climb over a wall or through a
window. No, Jesus is the only gate through which we can
enter the kingdom of Heaven.

You will want to be on the inside when that gate is locked.

*There will be weeping and gnashing of teeth, when ye shall
see Abraham, and Isaac, and Jacob, and all the prophets, in
the kingdom of God, and you yourself thrust out.*

Luke 13:28

Do not let the distraction of your life keep you off the path
that leads through the Strait Gate. Jesus is the gate. Seek him,
and you will find him. You cannot get to the Father lest you
go through the Son.

THE BANK

Where did you leave Jesus?

Did you leave him at THE BANK?

And a certain ruler asked him, saying, Good master, what shall I do to inherit eternal life?

Thou knowest the commandments, Do not commit adultery, Do not kill, Do not steal, Do not bear false witness, Honor thy father and thy mother.

And he said, All these have I kept from my youth up.

Now when Jesus heard these things, he said unto him, Yet lackest thou one thing: sell all that thou hast, and distribute unto the poor, and thou shalt have treasure in heaven: and come, follow me.

And when he heard this, he was very sorrowful: for he was very rich.

Luke 18:18, 20-23

Ask yourself this question. Does the bank hold your treasures...all you hold dear, the security for your future? Oh, my friend, think again. You came into this world without anything, and you will leave the same way. The only treasure any of us have is in Jesus. The Bible tells us not to lay our treasure up here on earth.

Lay not up for yourselves treasures upon earth, where moth and rust doth corrupt, and where thieves break through and steal. But lay up for yourselves treasures in Heaven, where neither moth nor rust doth corrupt, and where thieves do not break through nor steal: For where your treasure is, there your heart will be also.

Matthew 6:19-21

Make sure your heart and your treasure are in Heaven, for there will be no need for banks in Heaven.

PRIDE

Where did you leave Jesus?

Did you leave Jesus in
FAVOR of your PRIDE?

Are you too proud of yourself and your accomplishments? Do you believe your sins are less than those of your neighbor?

Now when the Pharisee which had bidden him saw it, he spake within himself, saying, This man, if he were a prophet, would have known who and what manner of woman this is that toucheth him: for she is a sinner.

And Jesus answering said unto him, Simon, I have somewhat to say unto thee.

And he saith, Master, say on.

And he turned to the woman, and said unto Simon, Seest thou this woman? I entered into thine house, thou gavest me no water for my feet: but she hath washed my feet with tears, and wiped them with the hairs of her head.

Luke 7:39, 40, 44

YOUR SORROW

Where did you leave Jesus?

Could it be you left him in YOUR SORROW?

What are you sorrowing for right now? The loss of someone you love. The loss of a job, a home, finances, a friend. Whatever you have lost, JESUS is your answer. He is a friend that sticks closer than a brother. He will never leave you.

A man that hath friends must shew himself friendly: and there is a friend that sticketh closer than a brother.

Proverbs 18:24

When the world tells you that you have lost it all and there is nowhere else to turn, it is time to turn to Jesus. He never changes. He is the same yesterday, today, and tomorrow. Jesus is, was, and will be all you ever need.

Let your conversation be without covetousness; and be content with such things as ye have: for he hath said, I will never leave thee, nor forsake thee.

Hebrews 13:5

PILATE

Where did you leave Jesus?

Did you leave him before PILATE?

As Jesus stood before Pilate and his accusers, did you stand there in fear, saying let him "defend himself?" "I can't say anything in his defense for fear of the law of the land. Crucify him!" … When you say nothing, that is what you say.

And Pilate, when he had called together the chief priests and the rulers and the people, said unto them, Ye have brought this man unto me, as one that perverteth the people; and, behold, I, having examined him before you, have found no fault in this man touching those things whereof ye accuse him:

And they cried out all at once, saying, Away with this man, and release unto us Barabbas:

Pilate therefore, willing to release Jesus, spake again to them.

But they cried, saying, Crucify him, Crucify him.

Luke 23:13-14, 18, 20-21

GARDEN

Where did you leave Jesus?

Did you leave him in the GARDEN?

Perhaps you left him in the garden of Gethsemane. Maybe you've become weary from the trials of your life. Do you find yourself sleeping when you could be praying? You might say, "It's all right, Jesus can do it."

He did, and now he wants us to do the same.

What a gesture of love it is when we intercede for others in Jesus' name.

Keep in mind, drops as of blood poured from him for you, as your sins were laid upon him.

Then cometh Jesus with them unto a place called Gethsemane, and saith unto the disciples, Sit ye here, while I go and pray yonder.

Then saith he unto them, My soul is exceeding sorrowful, even unto death: tarry ye here and watch with me.

And he went a little farther, and fell on his face, and prayed, saying, O my father, if it be possible, let this cup pass from me: nevertheless, not as I will, but as thou wilt.

Matthew 26:36, 38-39

LAST SUPPER

Where did you leave Jesus?

Did you leave him at the LAST SUPPER?

Are you guilty of partaking of the "Bread of Life" and then leaving the celebration without a thought of what it cost "your host?"

And he took the cup and gave thanks, and said, Take this, and divide it among yourselves: For I say unto you, I will not drink of the fruit of the vine, until the kingdom of God shall come.

And he took bread, and gave thanks, and break it, and gave unto them, saying, This is my body which is given for you: this do in remembrance of me.

Likewise, also the cup after supper, saying, This cup is the new testament in my blood, which is shed for you.

But, behold, the hand of him that betrayeth me is with me on the table.

Luke 22:17-21

Ask yourself, "Am I guilty of partaking and then just leaving?"

THE CROSS

Where did you leave Jesus?

Have you left him on the CROSS?

Did you say goodbye to him and leave as he hung on the cross? *Just another dying man,* you might think. But you are so wrong!

He was and is your SAVIOR.

He did not have to, but he hung there for you and me. In your daily life, do you ever stop and thank him for giving his life so that you might have a life to live? A life to live FOR him here and WITH him throughout eternity.

And it was about the sixth hour, and there was a darkness over all the earth until the ninth hour.

And the sun was darkened, and the veil of the temple was rent in the midst.

And when Jesus had cried with a loud voice he said, Father, into thy hands I commend my spirit: and having said thus, he gave up the ghost.

Luke 23:44-46

THE TOMB

Where did you leave Jesus?

Did you leave him in the TOMB?

He died there on the cross, you say. And he did. They took him away and placed him in a tomb. That was what they did with all dead men. But remember, Jesus is not just another dead man.

Jesus said, "Destroy this temple, and in three days I will raise it up."

HE HAS RISEN!

And the angel answered and said unto the women, Fear not ye: for I know that ye seek Jesus, which was crucified. He is not here: for he is risen, as he said. Come, see the place where the Lord lay. And go quickly, and tell his disciples that he is risen from the dead; and, behold, he goeth before you into Galilee; there shall ye see him: lo, I have told you.

And they departed quickly from the sepulcher with fear and great joy; and did run to bring his disciples word. And as they went to tell his disciples, behold, Jesus met them, saying, All hail." And they came and held him by the feet, and worshiped him.

Then said Jesus unto them, Be not afraid: go tell my brethren that they go into Galilee, and there shall they see me.

Matthew 28:5-10

So, do not leave Jesus at the tomb...for he isn't there!

THE GREAT COMMISSION

Then the eleven disciples went away into Galilee, into a mountain where Jesus had appointed them. And when they saw him, they worshipped him: but some doubted.

And Jesus came and spake unto them, saying, All power is given unto me in heaven and in earth. Go ye therefore, and teach all nations, baptizing them in the name of the Father, and of the Son, and of the Holy Ghost: teaching them to observe all things whatsoever I have commanded you: and, lo, I am with you always, even unto the end of the world. Amen.

Matthew 28:16-20

Jesus is saying, "Be not afraid. I am with you always. I have not and will not leave you. I am with you right now, by the Holy Spirit. Go to the ends of the earth telling people about me. I am proclaiming you to My Father. Now you proclaim me to the world."

IN HEAVEN

Where did you leave Jesus?

Have you left him in HEAVEN?
Somewhere in the "great beyond?"

Too far away to reach him or have him reach you. No, Jesus said, I am going away, but if I go, I will send a comforter in MY place.

THE PROMISE OF THE SPIRIT

If ye love me, keep my commandments. And I will pray the Father, and he shall give you another Comforter, that he may abide with you for ever; even the Spirit of truth; whom the world cannot receive, because it seeth him not, neither knoweth him: but ye know him; for he dwelleth with you, and shall be in you.

I will not leave you comfortless: I will come to you. Yet a little while, and the world seeth me no more; but ye see me: because I live, ye shall live also. At that day ye shall know that I am in my Father, and ye in me, and I in you.

John 14:15-20

He is as far away as Heaven, yet as close as you, the temple, for YOU are the Temple of the Holy Spirit. Do not leave him. Invite him to come live in you right now.

He is just waiting for your invitation.

Do not leave him.

NO MATTER WHERE

NO MATTER WHERE YOU LEFT JESUS,

In the **MANGER**
At the **TEMPLE**
In **NAZARETH**
At the **WELL**
In the **VALLEY** of **INDECISION**
At the **GATE CALLED STRAIGHT**
At the **BANK**
In **FAVOR** of your **PRIDE**
In **YOUR SORROW**
Before **PILATE**
In the **GARDEN**
At the **LAST SUPPER**
On **THE CROSS**
In the **TOMB**
In **HEAVEN**

Wherever you left Jesus, GO BACK and get him! He is still there waiting for you.

Remember, he did not leave...YOU DID!

If you have never met Jesus, now is the time. He will meet you where you are, whether in a good place or a bad place. He doesn't care where you meet Him, only that you meet Him.

If you do not know Jesus as your personal Lord and Savior, pray this prayer sincerely from your heart.

Heavenly Father,

I am a Sinner. I believe Jesus is your son.

I believe you sent Jesus to die in my place for my sins. I believe he died and rose again.

I ask you to forgive me of my sins, and I ask Jesus to come into my heart and life. Cleanse me and make me whole. I pronounce you Lord of my life.

Father, from this day forward, I will live for you.

In Jesus name,

Amen!

If you just sincerely prayed that prayer, you are a new creation in Christ Jesus, and your name is written in Heaven in the Lamb's Book of Life!

Congratulations! You have just made the most important decision of your life!

NOTES

NOTES

NOTES

NOTES

NOTES

NOTES

www.ingramcontent.com/pod-product-compliance
Lightning Source LLC
Chambersburg PA
CBHW051334150726
47997CB00004B/1464